SHARKS!

tiger tales

5 River Road, Suite 128, Wilton, CT 06897
Published in the United States 2022
Text by Lauren Crisp
Photographic images courtesy of www.shutterstock.co.uk
Text and illustrations copyright © 2022 Little Tiger Press Ltd.
ISBN-13: 978-1-6643-4037-4
ISBN-10: 1-6643-4037-8
Printed in China
LTK/2700/1098/0122

www.tigertalesbooks.com

The world is an ever-changing place, and the people within it are capable of incredible things: discoveries are made, records are broken, new facts are found, and history recovered. We will be happy to revise and update information in future editions.

SHARKS!

tiger tales

WHAT ARE SHARKS?

Sharks are a **type of fish**, but they are not just any fish! What makes sharks **different?**

SKELETON

Most fish have a skeleton made of bone, but a shark's entire skeleton is made of **cartilage**.

Try wiggling your nose and see how it moves really easily—that is cartilage! This is how sharks **twist**, **turn**, and **bend** so quickly and easily.

TEETH

When a shark dies, its cartilage skeleton rots, so usually the only evidence that a shark ever existed is its **teeth**, which turn into **fossils**.

Sharks have many rows of teeth so that every time one is lost, another takes its place. A shark can go through more than 20,000 **teeth** during its life!

SKIN

While fish are covered in scales, sharks have little "teeth" all over their bodies called **dermal denticles**, which point in the same direction.

If you were to rub a shark from its head to its tail, it would feel really smooth. If you rubbed it the other way, it would feel very rough, like sandpaper.

Dermal denticles allow a shark to cut through water and **swim much faster.**

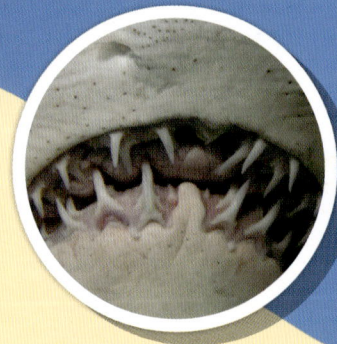

BABIES

Most fish lay eggs in the sea, but sharks have three different ways of having babies (called **pups**) depending on what type of shark they are:

1 By **laying eggs** and leaving them somewhere safe until they hatch.

2 By **holding the babies** inside their body even after the eggs hatch, so that the pups can grow bigger and stronger inside the mother before they are born.

3 By **giving birth** to live baby sharks, just like mammals do.

Shark eggs can look different. Some look like a soft pouch, called a **mermaid's purse**. Others are shaped like a **corkscrew**.

Mother sharks don't often take care of their babies, so it's a good thing that the pups are born with a full set of **sharp teeth**!

There are more than **400 species** of shark!

Most sharks **never sleep**! They must constantly move forward to allow water to flow through their gills so they can breathe. They do need to rest once in a while, though.

MEGALODON SHARK TOOTH

Fossilized shark teeth show that sharks have existed for more than **400 million years**, making them older than the **dinosaurs**!

DID YOU

Some sharks can **glow in the dark**!

The largest shark ever discovered, at around 50 feet (15 m) long and with 7-inch- (18-cm-) long teeth, was called the **Otodus megalodon** shark. It has been extinct for 3.6 million years!

Most sharks have five different types of fin, which provide balance and stability, making them **super-swimmers!**

SHARK FIN

Sharks have an amazing sense of **hearing.** They can hear prey up to 800 feet (250 m) away.

KNOW?

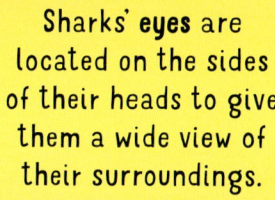

Sharks' **eyes** are located on the sides of their heads to give them a wide view of their surroundings.

Sharks cannot swim **backward.**

The **smallest** known shark is the dwarf lantern shark, at about 6 inches (15 cm) long. The **largest** is the whale shark that grows to around 40 feet (12 m) long.

GREAT WHITE SHARK

The great white shark is a super-efficient and deadly hunter.

At any one time, a great white shark has around 300 sharp, serrated **teeth**, which can grow to around 2 inches (5 cm) long.

It eats fish, sea lions, and dolphins, but its favorite food is **seals**. It surprises its prey by sneaking up from below the surface of the water!

WARNING!

SHARK SIGHTED

Humans aren't on a great white shark's menu, but sometimes a shark mistakes a person for a seal and takes a "**sample bite**." Attacks on people are really a case of mistaken identity!

Fasten your **flippers**, hold on tight.

The **great white shark** just loves to **bite!**

Watch out for shark fins!

The great white likes to swim in **shallow** waters, near the surface.

With no known ocean-living predators other than the **orca** (also known as the killer whale), the great white is truly the **king of the sharks!**

A great white can detect a single drop of **blood** in a bathtub full of water. It can even sense the **heartbeat** of another living creature!

STATS

Size: Up to 20 ft (6 m)

Weight: Up to around 5,000 lbs (2,300 kg)

Speed: Around 15 mph (24 kph)

Life expectancy: Up to 70 years

Habitat: Cool, coastal waters around the world

WHALE SHARK

The whale shark is the largest known fish in the world.

The whale shark is not actually a whale (which is a mammal), but it is as **big** as some whales.

It has an **enormous** mouth that stretches about 3 to 5 feet (1 to 1.5 m) wide. **Say cheese!**

The whale shark has a mouth full of very small teeth. It doesn't need big teeth because it doesn't hunt its prey. Instead, it swims along very slowly, with its **wide mouth open**, feeding on tiny fish, fish eggs, and plankton—like a living **vacuum cleaner!**

Plankton are really tiny marine organisms—or living things—that float around in the water.

The whale shark has a mouth that's **wide.**

Dive right in and **hitch a ride!**

Known as the **gentle giant** of the sea, divers often hitch a ride with the whale shark!

The markings on a whale shark...

...are as **unique** as human fingerprints!

! BIG SHARK

STATS

Size: Up to 40 ft (12 m)

Weight: Up to around 40,000 lbs (18,000 kg)

Speed: Around 3 mph (5 kph)- roughly human walking speed

Life expectancy: 70-100 years

Habitat: Warm waters around the world

It loves swimming in **warm, tropical oceans.**

MAKO SHARK

The mako shark is the fastest species of shark yet discovered.

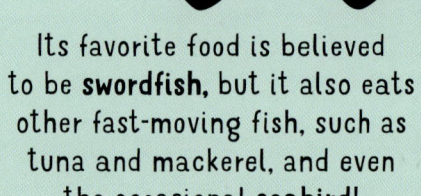

Its favorite food is believed to be **swordfish**, but it also eats other fast-moving fish, such as tuna and mackerel, and even the occasional **seabird!**

The mako shark is super-fast.

There's no chance it will come in last!

The mako can also **jump** incredibly high—they have been known to leap 20 feet (6 m) or more onto the decks of boats! When a shark jumps out of the water, this is called a **breach**.

WARNING!

JUMPING SHARKS

Swimming at 30 mph (48 kph) is common for the mako shark. If it is in a **hurry**, it can reach 45 mph (72 kph)!

It has the biggest **brain**, in proportion to its body size, of any shark. This just might make the mako the **smartest shark** as well as the fastest.

45 mph

With its big eyes and excellent eyesight, streamlined body shape (known as **hydrodynamic**), and incredibly sharp teeth, the mako is a **fearsome ocean predator.**

STATS

Size: Up to around 13 ft (4 m)

Weight: Around 1,000 lbs (450 kg)

Speed: Top speeds of 45 mph (72 kph)

Life expectancy: Around 30 years

Habitat: Tropical waters around the world

HAMMERHEAD SHARK

The hammerhead shark has an unusually shaped head.

This shark has a long, flat head, shaped a little like a **hammer**—which is how it got its name.

It has **super-sharp**, triangular **teeth**, making this not only a strange-looking shark, but a **fierce** one!

Hammerhead at large!

Hammerheads swim together during the day in what are called **schools** and then go out on their own at night to hunt.

Hammerheads might look quite strange...

but they have **superior** visual range!

Its **eyes** are at the very outside ends of its head, allowing it to see almost everything around it in **all directions**.

Its favorite food is the **stingray**. Even if a stingray is completely hidden under the sand, the hammerhead uses special **electrical sensors** that are spread across its head to seek them out, pin them down, and gobble them up!

Hammerheads don't seem to be affected by the stingray's sting.

STATS

Size: Up to around 20 ft (6 m) long

Weight: Up to around 1,000 lbs (450 kg)

Speed: Up to 25 mph (40 kph)

Life expectancy: 20–30 years

Habitat: Warm walers around the world

The hammerhead rarely attacks humans. It just might show a little **curiosity** toward divers swimming in its home.

GREENLAND SHARK

The Greenland shark is the longest-living shark.

The Greenland shark can live for up to **400 years**!

This shark lives deep down in the coldest of seas, where temperatures are often below **freezing**.

Beware! Cold water

It swims very slowly—less than 1 mile per hour (1.6 kph)—through the chilly water.

The Greenland shark is perfectly adapted to cold water, with special **chemicals** in its body that keep ice crystals from forming. This chemical also happens to make this shark **poisonous** if eaten!

The Greenland shark enjoys the cold and lives to be extremely old!

The Greenland shark is often **blind** because of a pesky **parasite** that likes to attach itself to its eyes.

What this shark lacks in sight, it makes up for with its incredible sense of **smell**!

STATS

Size: Around 23 ft (7 m)

Weight: Up to around 2,000 lbs (900 kg)

Speed: Less than 1 mph (1.6 kph)

Life expectancy: Up to 400 years

Habitat: Freezing waters of the Arctic and North Atlantic Oceans

It will hunt and eat almost any fish or squid, but more often, it **scavenges** for its meals, like the body of a polar bear that has fallen through the ice, or the carcass of a whale.

THRESHER SHARK

The thresher shark uses its tail to stun its prey.

The thresher shark is believed to have the longest **tail fin** (also called the **caudal fin**) of all living sharks. It can be almost as long as its body!

Not only does this shark have a super-long tail, but it uses it to catch fish, which is thought to be **unique** to the thresher shark.

It swims into a school of fish and **whips** its tail at lightning speed, slapping the fish until they are completely **stunned**... then it's dinner time!

The thresher's tail can stun its prey.

It's best to keep out of its way!

Thrashing tails!

The thresher shark is a very fast swimmer and sometimes leaps right out of the water, using its tail to propel itself upward and perform athletic **twists** and **turns** in midair!

STATS

Size: Up to 20 ft (6 m)

Weight: Around 1,100 lbs (500 kg)

Speed: Up to 30 mph (48 kph)

Life expectancy: 20 years or more

Habitat: Tropical and temperate seas around the world

The thresher shark's favorite foods are mackerel, sardines, tuna, and squid.

NURSE SHARK

Nurse sharks are probably the most relaxed sharks in the ocean.

The nurse shark loves finding cozy hiding places under ledges or in **caves**, where it settles with other sharks.

Sometimes groups of up to 40 of these sharks are found in a huddle, just **lounging** the day away!

The **nurse shark** slumbers through the day

and wakes at night to **suck** its prey!

At night, the nurse shark leaves the group to go out on its own to **hunt**. For this, it uses its **barbels**, the dangling features on its face, which contain taste buds. The shark drags them along the seafloor to find food like sea urchins, squid, and shrimp, which it then sucks up into its mouth.

Most sharks need water to flow through their **gills** to breathe—they could actually drown if they don't keep moving! But the nurse shark is **different**, because it can pump water through its mouth and gills without having to swim.

The nurse shark lives a gentle, **quiet life**, but be warned: It will defend itself if threatened—and if it attaches its mouth to something, **it won't let go!**

It can even **slurp** a sea snail clean out of its shell!

STATS

Size: Up to around 10 ft (3 m)

Weight: Around 200–300 lbs (90–140 kg)

Speed: Around 1.5 mph (2.4 kph) but can go faster in short bursts

Life expectancy: 20-25 years

Habitat: Tropical waters of the Atlantic and Pacific Oceans

OCEANS OF STICKERS!

Place your stickers here.

WARNING!

SHARK
SIGHTED

STICKERS!